WITHDRAWN

You Are in Ancient China

Ivan Minnis

Raintree

Chicago, Illinois

© 2005 Raintree
Published by Raintree, a division of Reed
Elsevier, Inc.
Chicago, Illinois

Customer Service 888-363-4266

Visit our website at www.raintreelibrary.com

All rights reserved. No part of this publication
may be reproduced or transmitted in any form
or by any means, electronic or mechanical,
including photocopying, recording, taping,
or any information storage and retrieval system,
without permission in writing from the publisher.
For information, address the publisher:
Raintree,100 N. LaSalle, Suite 1200, Chicago,
IL 60602

Printed and bound in China by the South China
Printing Company

08 07 06 05
10 9 8 7 6 5 4 3 2

**Library of Congress
Cataloging-in-Publication Data**
Minnis, Ivan.
  You are in ancient China / Ivan Minnis.
    v. cm. -- (You are there)
  Audience: Ages 7-9.
  Includes index.
  Contents: A great civilization -- The ancient
Chinese -- Life in the country -- Chinese cities --
Food and drink -- Growing up in ancient China --
Reading and writing -- Chinese art -- Science and
technology -- Festivals and entertainment --
Emperors and officials -- Religion and beliefs --
Facts for ancient Chinese.
  ISBN 1-4109-0619-1 (library binding-hardcover) -
- ISBN 1-4109-1011-3 (pbk.)
  1. China--Civilization--221 B.C.-960 A.D.--
Juvenile literature. [1. China--Civilization--221
B.C.-960 A.D. 2. China--Social life and customs--
221 B.C.-960 A.D.] I. Title. II. You are there
(Chicago, Ill.)
DS748.13.M56 2005
931--dc22
                                  2003027642

Acknowledgments
The author and publishers are grateful to the
following for permission to reproduce copyright
material: p. 5, 9, 27 Debbie Rowe; p. 6 Ancient Art
& Architecture/J.F. Kenney; p. 7, 11, 19, 22
Werner Forman Archive; p. 8, 25 British Museum;
p. 10, 16 Ancient Art & Architecture/William
Lindesay; p. 12, 15 Art Archive; p. 13 Sally and
Richard Greenhill; p. 14 Smithsonian
Institute/Freer Gallery of Art and Arthur M Sackler
Gallery; p. 17 Bridgeman Art Library/Bibliotheque
Nationale, Paris; p. 18 AKG Images/Erich Lessing;
p. 21 Art Archive/Bibliotheque Nationale, Paris; p.
23 Michael Holford; p. 24 Corbis; p. 26, 28, 29
Ancient Art & Architecture/R. Sheridan.

The publisher would like to thank May-lee Chai
for her assistance in the preparation of this book.

Every effort has been made to contact copyright
holders of any material reproduced in this book.
Any omissions will be rectified in subsequent
printings if notice is given to the publisher.

Contents

Any words appearing in bold, **like this,** are explained
in the glossary.

A Great Civilization

The Chinese **civilization** has lasted for over 5,000 years. This is longer than any other civilization. Over 2,200 years ago, in 221 B.C.E., China became a united **empire.** It was ruled by **emperors** for over 2,000 years. The emperors stayed in power until 1912, less than 100 years ago.

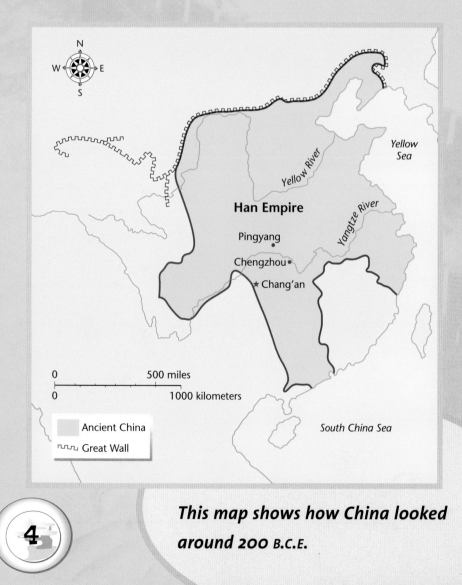

This map shows how China looked around 200 B.C.E.

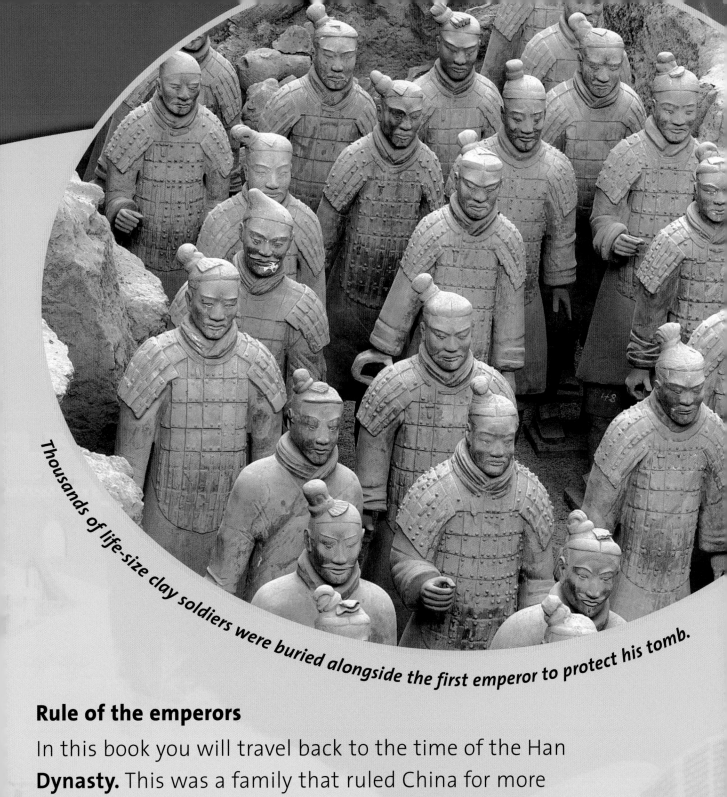

Thousands of life-size clay soldiers were buried alongside the first emperor to protect his tomb.

Rule of the emperors

In this book you will travel back to the time of the Han **Dynasty.** This was a family that ruled China for more than 400 years, from 207 B.C.E to 220 C.E. You will travel through the towns and countryside, learning what it was like to live in ancient China.

The Ancient Chinese

Imagine walking through the busy streets of an ancient Chinese city. Watch for carriages carrying government officials. Officials are dressed in beautiful **silk** robes. Only important people are allowed to wear silk. Even the merchants who sell silk are often not allowed to wear the clothes themselves.

Other wealthy people also wear beautiful robes. They wear shoes with curled toes. The women wear expensive jewelry. You can see green jewelry made from jade. Wealthy women decorate their hair with pretty pins. Men and women who do not have to work grow their fingernails very long. Long fingernails show others that the person is wealthy.

Most people in China have to walk to get places. Officials travel by horse or carriage.

Jewelry is worn by wealthy people in China. This pendant is made from jade.

Work clothes

Most working people are dressed very differently from wealthy people. Both men and women wear short, plain robes and flat sandals. These clothes are better for people who work hard in the fields. In cold weather, people add padding between different layers of robes to keep warm.

Life in the Country

Most Chinese people live in the countryside. Most families own their small farms, but they must pay part of what they earn or grow to a local **noble.** This payment is called a **tax.**

In the north of China, the weather is dry, so the people grow wheat and other grains. They also grow vegetables and keep pigs and chickens. Although oxen are used to pull the heavy plows, most of the work is done by hand.

This is a pottery model of a sheep pen from the Han Dynasty.

Even today, people in China still work the rice fields mostly by hand.

The rice harvest

Everywhere you look in southern China, people are growing rice. Rice grows best in flooded fields. **Canals** are dug so that water can be carried from the large rivers to flood the fields. A good rice harvest is very important. A bad harvest can mean there is not enough food to go around. The whole family helps to bring in the rice, even little children.

Learning about farms

Farming was so important that the ancient Chinese left many pictures and models that tell us about their farms. In many parts of China, farming has hardly changed at all. Rice is still grown the same way today as it was 2,000 years ago.

Chinese Cities

China has some of the biggest and busiest cities in the ancient world. The towns and cities are surrounded by high walls to protect them. China is so big that it is hard for the **emperor** to rule it well. In each city, government officials make sure that everyone follows the emperor's orders. These officials live in a special part of the town.

Cities are surrounded by high walls and watchtowers to protect them from attack.

This is the tomb of Emperor Gao Zong and Empress Wu, near Chang'an.

Business and markets

In the big cities each different business has its own street. All the streets are centered around a huge marketplace. The buildings can be three or four stories high. People travel from the country to buy and sell their goods in the city. They are amazed by the high walls and huge buildings. Most of the buildings are made of wood. This is very dangerous because fire can spread quickly from one building to another.

Learning about cities: Xi'an

Xi'an is an ancient city in China. Chang'an, the **capital** city of the Han **empire,** was very close to modern Xi'an. Many buildings remain from ancient times, as well as the strong city wall. Xi'an is still one of the largest cities in China today.

Food and Drink

If you live in the country, most of your meals will include rice. That is why the rice harvest is so important. Rice can be made into cakes, porridge, and dumplings. It can be **brewed** to make wine.

Most people rarely eat meat. In coastal areas and along rivers, fish are caught for food. Cattle are not common in China. This means that you will rarely eat dairy products such as milk and cheese. Everything is cooked in a pot called a ding. The ding pot has three legs so the pot can be put on top of the fire. The food can cook more quickly this way.

Landowners hire people to watch the peasants working in the fields.

Patterned bowls like these are used for serving food.

China tea

The ancient Chinese were the first people to drink tea. For many years tea was used as a medicine. By about 100 B.C.E. it was being grown all over China. Both rich and poor people drink tea with meals. Powdered leaves are soaked in boiling water, making a delicious drink. There are many different flavors of tea, and some are very expensive.

Children in China

You will probably find that in ancient China, people live in the same house as their grandparents, parents, aunts and uncles, brothers, sisters, and cousins. This is called an extended family. Respect and honor are important to Chinese families. Everyone is expected to obey the oldest male member of the family. Children are taught to respect their elders and their **ancestors.**

Wealthy children are often looked after by nannies. These children are having a bath.

Chinese boys study hard to pass the tests to become officials for the emperor.

Working and studying

In poor families children are expected to work hard. Boys help their fathers in the fields. Girls learn to cook, sew, weave cloth, and help with chores. At harvest time everyone works in the fields. Wealthy children also grow up in large families, but their lives are very different. Boys go to school to learn to read and write so that they can become one of the **emperor's** officials.

Girls in rich families usually stay at home to learn from their mothers. They learn how to run a home. Parents usually arrange marriages for their children. All this does not leave much time for playing, but board games similar to chess are popular. Some families keep small pets, like birds and crickets.

Since you are used to the English alphabet, you will find the Chinese language very difficult to learn. There are nearly 50,000 different **symbols.** When written together they make different sounds and words. If you want to become a government official you will need to learn at least 6,000 of these symbols.

Chinese symbols are read from top to bottom rather than left to right.

Learning about paper

One of the most important inventions of the ancient Chinese was paper. It was invented around 100 C.E. Fibers from a plant called hemp were soaked in water until they became a mushy pulp. A wooden frame with a fine mesh stretched across it was used to lift a thin layer of this pulp. Once it dried, it was a perfect surface for writing.

The first emperor wanted to change China, so he burned the writings of scholars.

People all over China speak different types of Chinese. They cannot understand each other when they speak. But people who have learned to read and write can all read the same symbols. This makes writing very important. The **emperor** sends his written words far and wide. The few people who can read them become very powerful.

Chinese Art

You will see beautiful works of art all over China, especially in the homes of the rich. Their houses are painted in bright colors. Everyday objects like serving dishes are shaped and painted. The **silk** robes of the rich are dyed with many colors and decorated with patterns.

The artists

Chinese writing is also very pretty. The characters are often painted by special artists called calligraphers. They have a very skilled job and are greatly respected by the people. Many professional artists work for the **emperor.** Painting and **calligraphy** are also popular **hobbies** for wealthy people.

Chinese pots are often painted by skilled artists.

Learning about Chinese art

We can learn a lot about the ancient Chinese from their art. Carved and molded figures of people show us the clothes and hairstyles they wore. We can also learn a lot about their religious beliefs. Detailed figures and models were buried along with important people. This shows that they believed in an **afterlife.** The model figures would help to look after their master or mistress in the afterlife.

These models show two Chinese princesses. You can see the details of their patterned robes and hairstyles.

Science and Technology

The Chinese are famous for being great inventors and engineers. As you travel around China you will see wonderful inventions that you would not see anywhere else in the world. The engineers have created huge **canals** to carry goods and people across the country. They can also prevent the great rivers of China from flooding.

There are long and wide roads to travel on. These are designed for officials and armies to travel around the country. The middle lane is reserved for the **emperor** and his messengers.

ball

Earthquakes are very common in China. This is an earthquake detector. If the ground shakes at all, a ball drops into the frog's mouth.

Learning about Chinese inventions

Many of the things we use in the 21st century were first invented in ancient China. Here are some of them:

Around 3000 B.C.E. – **silk**

Around 600 B.C.E. – iron casting

205 B.C.E.–220 C.E. – ship rudders, wheelbarrows, compasses, glazed pottery, hot air balloons

130 C.E. – seismographs, for measuring earthquakes

700–800 C.E. – gunpowder discovered

Canals link the great rivers of China. They are used to transport goods and people across this huge country.

The Chinese have made great medical discoveries. Many of these will be in use for centuries. The doctors use herbs and **acupuncture** to cure illness. They also know that healthy eating is important.

Festivals and Entertainment

The ordinary people in China work in the fields all day and have very little time off. Everyone looks forward to the national festivals. The biggest festival in China is at the New Year. It marks the beginning of spring and the start of the farming year. Families gather together to exchange gifts. There are wonderful feasts and music and dancing.

These musicians are playing flutes and pipes for the Emperor.

This model shows two people wrestling. Acrobats and wrestlers entertain people at festivals.

Making music

Music is very popular. It is played on bamboo flutes and a stringed instrument called a ch'in. Drums and bells are also popular. Many rich families employ servants who are musicians. They play at **banquets** to entertain the family and their friends.

Educated Chinese people enjoy reading and writing poetry. The most famous poetry book is called the *Book of Songs*. Poor people also enjoy poetry and storytelling. They play games like chess and dice. Sometimes they watch acrobats and jugglers, but work leaves very little time for entertainment.

Emperors and Officials

China is ruled by an **emperor** but most of the people live thousands of miles from the **capital** city. There are no phones and few good roads so the emperor depends on his officials to run the country for him. There are thousands of officials all over China.

To work for the emperor you must pass difficult tests. These people must learn the works of the great thinker Confucius by heart, then answer questions about them on their test.

Much of the Great Wall of China was built during the Han Dynasty.

This instrument was used by the emperor or a general to call the armies.

Learning about the emperor

We know about rulers because many of the things they owned have survived. Many of their orders and instructions were written on paper and wood. The contents of their tombs show us their great wealth. We know that they used the dragon as their **symbol** from the very earliest times. Beautiful carvings and paintings of dragons appear on many of the emperors' belongings.

The emperor knows that it is important to keep his people safe from attack. Around 214 B.C.E. Emperor Qin Shi Huangdi completed the Great Wall to defend China from attacks from the north. The wall is still standing today.

Religion and Beliefs

Many of the religious beliefs of the ancient Chinese are based on the writings of Confucius. He was a great thinker who lived between 551 and 479 B.C.E. He taught that it was important for people to respect each other. He believed that not only must people respect their rulers, but the rulers must care for and respect the people.

Respecting your ancestors

Confucius said that the most important people to respect are the members of your family. Because of this most Chinese people worship and pray to their **ancestors.** People keep **shrines** to their ancestors in their homes.

Everyone in ancient China has heard of Confucius. Children learn his teachings in school.

Learning about beliefs

The ancient Chinese believed that when they died they needed to take things with them into the **afterlife.** The emperor Qin Shi Huangdi was buried with a huge army of **terracotta** soldiers. The life-sized figures are so detailed that no two soldiers have the same face.

The ancient Chinese believe that the army of statues buried with the first emperor will protect him in the afterlife.

Facts for Ancient China

Dates to remember:

Around **6000** B.C.E. The first farmers start to live in China's Yellow River Valley

551 B.C.E. Confucius, ancient China's greatest thinker, is born

221–207 B.C.E. Qin **Dynasty:** The first emperor Qin Shi Huangdi unites China

207 B.C.E.**–220** C.E. Han Dynasty

100 C.E. Papermaking invented

618–906 C.E. Tang Dynasty

960–1279 C.E. Song Dynasty

Money

○ The same bronze coins are used all over China. They were introduced by the emperor Qin Shi Huangdi in about 200 B.C.E. Each coin has a hole in the middle.

Chinese coins can be linked together on a string or belt for safekeeping.

Time

- The Chinese calendar has been used for over 4,600 years — since 2637 B.C.E — longer than any other calendar

- Each year is named after an animal: rat, ox, tiger, rabbit, dragon, snake, horse, sheep, monkey, rooster, dog, or boar. Each animal is repeated every 12 years.

This oracle bone is carved with symbols of the Chinese calendar.

Find Out for Yourself

You cannot actually travel back in time to ancient China but you can still find out a lot about the people and how they lived. You will find the answers to some of your questions in this book. You can also use other books and the Internet.

Books to read

Deedrick, Tami. *Ancient Civilizations: China*. Chicago: Raintree, 2001.

Pancella, Peggy. *Qin Shi Huangdi: First Emperor of China*. Chicago: Heinemann Library, 2004.

Using the Internet

Explore the Internet to find out more about ancient China. Websites can change, so if some of the links below no longer work, try using a kid-friendly search engine, such as www.yahooligans.com or www.internet4kids.com, and type in keywords such as "terracotta army," "Great Wall of China," "Confucius," and "ancient China."

Websites

www.pbs.org/wgbh/nova/lostempires/
This site offers information on many different ancient civilizations, including China.
www.mnsu.edu/emuseum/prehistory/china/
This site focuses on all time periods in ancient China. A helpful timeline is included.

Disclaimer
All the Internet addresses (URLs) given in this book were valid at the time of going to press. However, due to the dynamic nature of the Internet, some addresses may have changed, or sites may have ceased to exist since publication. While the author and publishers regret any inconvenience this may cause readers, no responsibility for any such changes can be accepted by either the author or the publishers.

Glossary

acupuncture   ancient system of Chinese medicine that uses needles in various parts of the body to cure diseases. Today acupuncture is widely practiced around the world.

afterlife   idea that people's souls continue to exist after the person has died

ancestor   person someone is descended from. For example, your great-grandfather is an ancestor of yours.

banquet   formal dinner for many people

brew   prepare by soaking in hot water

calligraphy   artistic style of writing

canal   man-made waterway for boats

capital   location of a government

civilization   the way of life of a group of people

dynasty   series of rulers from the same family

emperor   person who rules a group of people or countries

empire   group of people or countries under one ruler

hobby   activity done for fun

noble   person of very high birth or rank

shrine   place that is considered sacred or holy

silk   fine fiber spun by insect larvae that is used to create cloth

symbol   something that stands for something else

tax   money collected by the government from people

terracotta   brownish-orange clay used mostly for statues and vases

Index